GETTING PAID TO
Manage
Social Media

DON RAUF

ROSEN
PUBLISHING®

New York

Published in 2017 by The Rosen Publishing Group, Inc.
29 East 21st Street, New York, NY 10010

First Edition

Library of Congress Cataloging-in-Publication Data

Names: Rauf, Don, author.
Title: Getting paid to manage social media / Don Rauf.
Description: First edition. | New York : Rosen Publishing, 2017. | Series:
  Turning your tech hobbies into a career | Audience: Grades 7 to 12. |
  Includes bibliographical references and index.
Identifiers: LCCN 2016020616 | ISBN 9781508172949 (library bound)
Subjects: LCSH: Social media—Management—Vocational guidance—Juvenile
  literature. | Online social networks—Juvenile literature.
Classification: LCC HM851 .R387 2017 | DDC 302.23/1—dc23
LC record available at https://lccn.loc.gov/2016020616

Manufactured in Malaysia

Contents

Introduction

John Yembrick has his dream job. He is the social media manager for the National Aeronautics and Space Administration (NASA). He uses all the top social media tools such as Facebook, Twitter, Instagram, and Tumblr to help promote the US space program. Before astronaut Scott Kelly headed to the International Space Station for his record-breaking 340-day stay, Yembrick trained him on social media platforms to help publicize his mission.

Getting astronauts exposure through social media is good publicity. During one TweetChat, or Twitter conversation, President Barack Obama asked Kelly: "Do you ever look out the window and just freak out?" Kelly replied: "I don't freak out about anything, Mr. President. Except getting a Twitter question from you." The exchange gained attention in media around the world.

Yembrick has also hosted sessions with other social media programs such as Tumblr Answer Time, Google Hangouts, Reddit AMA ("Ask Me Anything") discussions, and Facebook Q&A. He recently started putting content on Snapchat. He continually posts content, whether it be an awesome new image of Earth from the International Space Station or a new photo of a distant galaxy from the Hubble Space Telescope.

"Whether it is through Twitter or Facebook or NASA.gov, we have this great way to connect with people directly that we never had before," said Yembrick in an interview with the author. "I have become a zealot for social media within NASA."

An interest in social media tools, such as Facebook, Twitter, and Instagram, can translate into a paying job and even a career.

Yembrick said that learning how to write and frame messaging with social media is a skill that you develop over time.

"You learn what connects with people," he said. "The good thing about social media is you get instant feedback. If you post something and it doesn't do well, you can see that. You have analytics and stats—retweets or shares—you can look at right away."

Yembrick sees plenty of opportunity for young people who want to get a job in social media. He said that young people today already have a lot of the social media skills that he had to learn.

"It's second nature to them," he said. "Even though social media is fun and something you use to communicate with your friends, it also could absolutely turn into a job because this is how people are sharing information in the twenty-first century."

Many employers know that young people understand social media and are willing to hire young people for entry-level positions in this area. So if you spend a lot of time online, it isn't necessarily time wasted. If you develop strong skills with Facebook, Twitter, Instagram, Snapchat, and other social media platforms, it can certainly lead to a way to make money. With some additional training and job-hunting skills, you could find a dream job like John Yembrick's that combines social media with your interests.

Chapter ONE
Social Media 101

Most of today's young people are very familiar with social media. They are constantly connected to Facebook, Snapchat, Twitter, Instagram, LinkedIn, YouTube, Vine, Google+, Tumblr,

Social media platforms, such as Snapchat (pictured), can be accessed through smartphones, making them easy to use from almost any location.

Pinterest, Reddit, and other online services. That's not to mention blogs, wikis (websites that provide collaborative modification of their content), internet forums, and podcasts.

Social media are tools, websites, and applications that people use to connect with others and create and share information, videos, and photos. Using these online tools, people build communities, interact, and collaborate. People interact with social media through their computers, smartphones, and tablets.

The whole social media world is relatively new. Facebook is just over a decade old. As a young technology, social media tend to be used more by young people than older people. When businesses use it, they are often trying to reach a young adult audience. The technologies are changing fast, too. Many students think that Facebook is already too old—they want the newest types of social media, so they have moved on to other sites such as Instagram and Snapchat.

Technology has certainly made it very easy for young people to spend tons of time on social media. Nine out of ten teens go online at least occasionally from a mobile device, according to a study from the Pew Research Center.

Certainly, social media use by young people has received negative press as well. It has been used for cyberbullying, and it can be a giant waste of time if not used properly. Some say it promotes narcissism because young people seem to post "selfies" nonstop on the web. Still, there can be a positive side. Some experts say that social media might help build self-confidence. A report from Common Sense media found that one in five teens said social media make them feel more confident. Many teens surveyed said they are more outgoing, less shy, and simply more social because of social media.

While many social media tools allow their users to be more outgoing and social, critics warn that they can promote negative behaviors, such as narcissism and cyberbullying.

And another major plus of mastering social media is that it can be a super valuable job skill. Today's businesses want to hire people who know how to reach people, promote their products, and build a loyal customer following, all through the social network.

TOP ENTERTAINERS KNOW HOW TO CONNECT

Do you want to see the power of social media? Take a look at some of today's top entertainers. Music superstar Beyoncé may be the queen when it comes to promotion using this technology. When the megastar was ready to release her recent album *Beyoncé,* she didn't turn to traditional advertising. She didn't tell a soul, and everyone involved with the project didn't say a word. Then shortly before Christmas, she sent a short message to her eight million Instagram followers that simply read "Surprise."

Many of today's most popular entertainers have mastered the power of social media. Beyoncé broke sales records after announcing the release of one of her albums on Instagram.

No one had any idea that she had an album coming out, but that was enough to get the buzz going.

Fans were excited and spread the word through Facebook and other social media outlets. The announcement sparked 1.2 million tweets in just twelve hours. As written in *Rolling Stone*, "Beyoncé made the internet explode." She gave Apple iTunes exclusive rights to release the fourteen songs and seventeen music videos. The album shattered iTunes store records with 828,773 albums sold in just three days. Talk about the power of social media! Beyoncé's campaign was off the charts.

Jimmy Fallon, host of *The Tonight Show*, is also a dynamo when it comes to using social media. He has more than thirty-nine million followers on Twitter and sends out his own tweets. Still, Fallon can't do it all alone. *The Tonight Show* has its own "director of social," Marina Cockenberg. Prior to this, she was the head blogger on the program in charge of original web content, as well as the day-to-day manager of the show's social platforms and long-term planning/creative web strategy.

Fallon not only sends out messages via Twitter, but he also gets a lot of his content through Twitter. He asks his fans to tweet funny anecdotes and use a hashtag to identify the topic. For example, he asked for funny short tales about moms. People wrote in using the hashtag #momtexts. A couple that he presented on air were: "@jimmyfallon My mom once texted me 'can you come over, I want you to take a selfie of me'" and "@jimmyfallon I once got a text from my mom where 'You're amazing' autocorrected to 'You're adopted.'" Fallon's extensive use of Twitter and other social media has led to a huge and loyal following. He even has a mascot who captures his love of social media: Hashtag the Panda.

Offbeat Social Networks

There are online communities for people with all sorts of interests. A site called VampireFreaks has 2.2 million members. On matchAdream, people discuss their nightly dreams.

Sometimes, a social media manager will want to target a specific audience, such as sports buffs, car enthusiasts, or even fans of vampires or people who love mustaches, for example. Here are a few more unique social networks of note:

- Goodreads is a social network geared toward bookworms.

- Ello bills itself as Facebook but without the ads.

- Twitch.tv is a platform built for gamers who want to share live streams of their gaming.

- SoundCloud may be the top social sound network for people who share music.

- Ravelry is a place for knitters, crocheters, designers, spinners, weavers, and dyers to keep track of their yarn, tools, and project and pattern information, and look to others for ideas and inspiration.

THE BASIC TOOLS TO MASTER

If you're totally new to the world of social media, here's a review of the big players and up-and-coming stars. The Pew Research Center recently surveyed more than one thousand teens ages thirteen to seventeen and found out their top social media platforms:

Facebook: 71 percent
Instagram: 52 percent
Snapchat: 41 percent
Twitter: 33 percent
Google+: 33 percent
Vine: 24 percent
Tumblr: 14 percent
Other social media sites: 11 percent

Even though teens are using more types of social media and some may be using Facebook less, Facebook is still the most popular site with young people.

FACEBOOK

Facebook is a social networking site where family and friends connect online. Mark Zuckerberg created it in 2004 when he was a student at Harvard University. Today, it has 1.65 billion users.

It is so popular because it is an easy way to share information with a large number of people. Many businesses have now established Facebook pages so customers can hear the latest news and offers. They also now advertise on Facebook because the network can help businesses reach the exact audience they want. Businesses can reach people based on location, age, gender, interests, and other factors.

INSTAGRAM

Instagram is a baby compared to Facebook, but it sure has been a fast-growing newbie. Started a few years after Facebook, Instagram focuses on photo and video sharing.

It quickly became a popular way for people to share images on their mobile devices of whatever they were doing—from eating a hot dog to dancing at a party to cheering at a sporting event. Instagram really helped popularize the "selfie" and became known for its beautiful photo formats. It offers ways to enhance images at the touch of a finger—you can add a vintage look, heighten the contrast, or make an image glow, for instance.

Big corporations have been reaching audiences through social networks. Coca-Cola uses Facebook, Twitter, Pinterest, and Google+, to name one example.

Instagram offers many different filters that bring different effects to the image.

Instagram's growth rate has been phenomenal. Two months after being introduced, Instagram had one million users. In 2012, it had more than one hundred million active users, and today it has more than four hundred million active users. Facebook admired its success so much that it eventually bought Instagram for $1 billion. Many businesses have started Instagram accounts and advertise on the platform as well.

SNAPCHAT

Snapchat is another story of fast success. Three students came up with the idea while taking a class at Stanford University in 2011 and launched it to the public that year. The app for mobile devices they created lets people send photos and videos, which then disappear for good a few seconds after they are viewed.

Teenagers especially have been big fans of Snapchat because it's not generally an app parents use, and the fact that their posts disappear after a short time ensures that their online lives are more private. Within a year of coming out, it had ten million users.

Recent statistics show that users send about two billion photos and videos per day via Snapchat. Recently, Snapchat introduced a service called Discover that allows companies and organizations to share content. The company has also presented other ways to advertise via the Snapchat app.

TWITTER

While people can post pictures and videos on Twitter, this social media tool is more about sending short messages. Some people compare Twitter to a conversation at a party—the bits of conversation are short.

The three hundred million–plus active Twitter users send and read short, up-to-140-character-long messages called "tweets." Why are the messages limited to 140 characters? Twitter is mostly used to send messages via mobile phones. The standard length of text messages is 160 characters. So when the founders launched Twitter in 2006, they set the character limit at 140.

This short-form messaging is an example of "microblogging." Blogs are websites where you can regularly update content, which is generally presented as posts. Typically, readers can comment on the material you post. Blogging is a great way to get fans or a customer base.

In addition to the "tweet," Twitter introduced the world to another new term: "hashtag." A hashtag is a "#" sign added to the beginning of an unbroken word or phrase in a tweet. A hashtag in a tweet links it to all the other tweets that include the hashtag sign along with the same word or phrase.

As with most social media tools, Twitter can be used by companies to gain followers. Social media managers use hashtags to bring Twitter users together in any ongoing conversation about a product, event, show, and more. Twitter offers advertising, too. Advertisers can target their ads to reach specific audiences—people in a certain age range or those who have specific interests, such as cars or sports.

GOOGLE+

Google+ (Google Plus) is similar to Facebook in many ways. While it has given Facebook some competition, most people still use Facebook, which is the giant in social media.

Google+ boasts about 111 million active users. Many fans like it because they are able to meet new people in different groups who share common interests.

TUMBLR

Tumblr is somewhat of a cross between a social networking site (like Facebook) and a blog (which is a regularly updated web page or site). Tumblr features mini-posts (for the most part) with text, images, or videos.

PINTEREST

Pinterest is similar to Tumblr in some regards because it's another way for people to share their interests and find others who have similar interests. Pinterest is called an online "pin board" or a visual social bookmarking site. A social bookmarking site is a service on the internet where users can store, organize, and share links to websites and web pages that are of interest to them. Digg and StumbleUpon are also popular bookmarking sites.

REDDIT

Reddit is another social media community that hundreds of millions of people use, including President Obama and Microsoft founder Bill Gates. Reddit users offer links to online content. Users can then vote on which content they think is important. (The name Reddit is basically a play on the words "read it," according to the Reddit Help section.)

Bill Gates, the founder of Microsoft, has appeared on Reddit "Ask Me Anything" sessions, answering questions on topics ranging from climate change to the future of human accomplishment.

OTHER NETWORKS

There are many other top networking tools as well. LinkedIn is designed to help people connect with others on matters related to business and careers. YouTube is the king of online videos. Vine is a mobile service that lets you capture and share short looping videos. It could be seen as the Twitter of video. An estimated one hundred million watch Vine videos every month.

New social media tools are emerging every year. Some succeed as businesses and some disappear. Several new ones are gaining steam, including Periscope (for broadcasting live video), Wanelo (a social shopping app), and WeChat (a texting and voice message service).

A PUBLIC APPETITE FOR APPS

Besides knowing the big-name platforms such as Facebook and Twitter, successful social media managers are familiar with related mobile apps as well.

These mobile apps are software applications developed specifically to use on small wireless devices, such as smartphones and tablets, instead of computers. For example, the Hootsuite app lets users see all their social channels in one place and monitor hashtags from a mobile device. This app allows a manager to be connected to all related social media at any place and time.

Pocket is an app that allows you to save articles and read them later. It lets you save posts from a mobile browser and read when you have time.

Evernote is another popular app that lets users save hashtags, keep blog ideas, and save anything on the web.

Chapter TWO

Learning the Basics

young people today often have a great advantage when it comes to social media. They are already very computer savvy. Many know all the functions of a mobile device. They often know a lot about social media because they use it so much. Just by regularly going on Facebook, Instagram, Snapchat, and Twitter, young people are building valued skills (although they might not

Young people who use social media a lot are actually building valuable skills. Those who master writing for online services are often in demand in the job market.

even know it). If you are someone who enjoys social media and wants to build upon what you might already know, there are several steps you can take.

WRITING SKILLS RULE

NASA's social media manager John Yembrick said in an interview with the author that building strong writing skills is essential to any job managing social media. "Learning how to write is really important in any communications job," he said.

Obviously, writing for social media is different from writing a school essay or book report. When you're writing for social media, it's often short, pithy, clever, and witty. If you're writing for social media, you have to stand out. There is a lot of competition for attention on screens across the world. You have to be compelling. If you wind up later in a company that is selling a product or service, you are often writing text that will show a reader a benefit to him or her.

Success is often measured according to how much a message is shared—so originality is key. People like to share something that is different and new. In jobs in this field, you want to write so people react and think: "I must share this with others." Also, unlike a formal paper for school, social media writing is more of a conversation.

No matter what, writing as much as possible and learning how to write well will be an enormous help in this field.

CHECK WITH YOUR SCHOOL

Schools may give students opportunities to use social media and hone talents with this modern technology. Increasingly,

Students can look for opportunities to sharpen their social media talents through classroom projects or by developing online campaigns to help their school.

schools are incorporating social media into their classwork. Some teachers are establishing Facebook pages to post items of interest that relate to coursework. Others provide real-time discussions with experts. While sitting in class, students may connect live with artists, politicians, scientists, athletes, and more—all through the right internet tools.

Some schools are already offering specific courses in social media. For example, the Weber School District in Utah has taught a class called Social Media Marketing for students in grades ten, eleven, and twelve. The purpose of the course has been to show how these new digital and social media tools are used in the world of business.

Other high schools that have given social media classes include Choctawhatchee High School in Fort Walton Beach, Florida, and Elkhorn Area High School in Wisconsin. St. John Vianney High School in St. Louis, Missouri, has a program that prepares young people for real-life careers by showing how social media strategies can be constructed and implemented and how to measure the effectiveness of social media.

Freehold High School in Western Monmouth County, New Jersey, has a medical science learning center, a culinary academy, and a computer science academy. On campus, students are encouraged to use their cell phones and other mobile devices for Twitter, Skype (a service for making video and audio calls over the internet), and a host of other social networking tools designed to help students market themselves.

Even if your school does not offer specific social media classes, other related courses can help, and many of them will have a segment devoted to social media. Check if your school provides classes in journalism, communications, public relations, advertising, or marketing.

DIY: MAKE YOUR OWN SOCIAL MEDIA

If no social media classes exist in your school already, you may be able to take the initiative and pursue the topic on your own, finding practical ways to apply the technology that will help your school. For example, your high school may not have a social media presence at all. You can discuss with a teacher or administrator how you might establish a school Facebook, Instagram, or Twitter account. If the school already has social media for itself, you can ask to play a role. Make suggestions on how to improve usage and boost school spirit.

Often, schools have special events to push school spirit, such as days when students wear pajamas, school colors, hats, costumes, and more. Getting the word out on these events can be difficult, but if more students sign up on school social media sites, events can be promoted through these tools. Plus, social media sites are a handy way to advertise school sporting events, plays, and concerts.

Be sure to take a lot of photos during any school event and post them online because people love to see themselves in photos, make comments, and interact with other users. Students typically share posts that feature them and their friends. Continual new content keeps people coming back to the school social media accounts. Here are five social media ideas that can help promote student involvement:

Ask Students to Vote. Have students vote on various topics. What should the school mascot be called? What should the theme of the prom be? What color should they paint the cafeteria? Do you think school should begin later in the morning? What should be the playlist for the school dance?

Poll Students on Real Issues. Social media can be used to gather opinions from the student body on political, social, and newsworthy topics. Who do you want to see elected as president of the United States? Do you think your school is doing enough to help the environment? Do you think speed limits should be lower?

Share Academic Help Sources. Students may need some academic help along the way, and a school Facebook page can provide ways to connect with tutors and other academic resources (helpful websites, etc.). Plus, a student may post a specific question about a class or problem. It's possible to get help from fellow students on potential college choices, homework problems, best places to study, or where to go on the weekend for entertainment (a public concert or opening of a Star Wars movie, maybe?).

Crowdsourcing information is one of the great functions of social media. This means you reach out to members who belong to a platform and ask their opinions. A student using a school Facebook page might ask where to get an affordable textbook or the best slice of pizza in town. Post a question and the responses will roll in from the crowd on the Facebook page.

Fundraise. Middle schools and high schools are often trying to raise money for different projects from taking school trips to spiffing up the bathrooms. Social media can be a great way to get out the word, encourage people to donate, and keep people up to date on the progress of any campaign.

Have Fun. Keeping a sense of fun is always helpful for promoting school spirit and blowing off steam after a long day of studying. Online, schools can give students a break with entertaining websites, interesting science photos, and trivia quizzes, just to name a few ideas.

Interning to the Top

As with most jobs, nothing pays off better than learning hands-on skills. One of the best approaches for a student is take an internship. Colleges offer internships, which allow a student the opportunity to work and train in a real business and learn from professionals. Students can typically earn credit by interning, and some internships even pay a small stipend.

LinkedIn, InternMatch, and Internships.com list social media intern jobs. Interns help establish and maintain a social media presence for a variety of companies from insurance firms to sports teams to tech startups. An intern may write new posts, track new leads gathered from Facebook or Twitter, report on how well an announcement was received, or suggest ideas for expanding the reach of a company through the latest social media tools.

Some of the best internships are competitive, so hone as many of your social media skills as you can before applying and know that you might have to complete an assignment to land the gig. For example, the New York Mets have asked their intern applicants to create a social campaign to help push a few Mets into the All-Star Game. High school may not be too early for some internships. Facebook has started recruiting high school students for its internship programs to stay ahead of the competition. Internships help students learn "soft skills" that can be valuable in any job. These include teamwork, communication, problem solving, leadership, and professional attitude. If you can't find organizations that are seeking volunteers, consider approaching groups that

GO ONLINE TO LEARN THE ROPES

The internet provides a wealth of material on how to use social media in job situations. Lynda.com encourages people

to check out its tutorials for social media marketing in a free trial period. Although much of the material out there can be advanced, you might want to look into material at Alison.com and HootSuite.com.

Hootsuite, for example, presents an introduction to social media marketing with an examination of Facebook, Twitter, LinkedIn, Instagram, YouTube, and Tumblr. To make sure the user is learning the material, quizzes are presented along with a page for community discussion. Besides an introduction course, the company covers more advanced topics such as how to grow your online community and master social advertising fundamentals.

FOLLOW A HIGHER EDUCATION

If you seriously want to master social media skills after graduating high school, colleges are now teaching programs in

Internships and volunteer programs can provide real workplace experience that can be crucial to landing a job down the road.

the subject. Because social media marketing is one of the most sought-after skills in companies today, some schools are focusing on how to master these tools to pursue a career.

Rutgers University in New Brunswick, New Jersey, has set up a "Mini-MBA" program in social media marketing. This certificate program helps participants design, manage, and track social media campaigns. At Austin Community College in Texas, students can invest two years of their time and emerge with a certificate in social media communications. Sometimes the social media portion will be part of a larger program. Online students with the University of Florida can pursue a master's degree in mass communication and have

Many colleges, such as Rutgers University (pictured), are now offering courses for those who are serious about taking their social media skills to the next level.

a specialization in social media. Southern New Hampshire University teaches an online bachelor's degree program in social media marketing.

Syracuse University has offered Social Media U Need 2 Know and COM 600 Social Media Theory and Practice. William Ward, who has taught a social media course there, has said in *Forbes* magazine that those who harness social communications are in high demand and have an advantage. Gradually, more major universities and colleges have been incorporating these media skills into their curriculum, including New York University, Columbia University, and the University of Washington.

While many college programs can be useful, many employers say that there is nothing like hands-on experience. Any opportunity to set up social media accounts for businesses or charities can be valuable experience, for example.

Chapter THREE

Building Your Social Media Chops

Managing social media brings together several distinct skills. These include creativity, writing, planning, organization, and some technical smarts. Ultimately, the goal of many social media experts is to generate business leads or fans. For businesses, the goal is often to turn these connections into sales and generate revenue. Sometimes, you might simply be trying to build a bigger audience to keep people returning to a website. Websites that have many consistent viewers can attract advertisers, and advertisers help businesses make money.

CONTENT IS KING

Although general writing skills are important, effective social media messaging is key to building an audience. One of the main features of social media messaging is that it's short. As with writing advertising copy, these messages have to grab attention.

Viewers are bombarded with information daily, so effective social media messaging is quick, to the point, and catchy.

Originality is important. Often you'll need to write a headline that grabs attention. Your content should not be boring or cause someone to respond with "this is the same old, same old."

You have to constantly think about what will engage your viewers. Sometimes this means being provocative to get viewers to click through to your site. Have you ever seen a post that shows an interesting photo and a headline that says something like "You won't believe what happens next?" That's meant to intrigue the user so he or she wants to find out more.

In other instances, you might try to trigger an emotional response. When a post makes people feel happy, for example, it can spread like wildfire. (How many posts featuring cute animals

To gain attention and keep viewers returning to a site, a social media manager has to produce content that is fresh, intriguing, and to the point.

have been shared millions of times?) If someone who views your social media copy takes action, then you know your content has worked, and you've done your job.

Some experts say that questions can be effective. Because you want people to react and respond, content is often in the form of a question. "The Acme Potato Chip Company wants to know: What is your favorite flavor of chip?" or "What do you think would be a winning new flavor for a chip?" People tend to answer questions, and that generates more engagement.

Speaking directly to the audience also has an impact. Sometimes telling people what to do works, such as "Click here now" or "Please retweet." The viewer may follow the command and visit your company website.

Having a consistent voice or personality also helps build an audience. People get to know your writing style and want to return to something they are familiar with. Paying attention to details pays off, too. Making a typo or providing a wrong price on a product that is for sale can ruin a social media campaign, as can an accidental tweet or Facebook message.

No matter what content needs to be written, time management is essential. As in most businesses, projects have to be well organized to meet deadlines. So no matter what you may wind up writing in the world of social media, always make sure you plan ahead to get the job done on time.

MEASURING REACH AND RESPONSE

Once you learn how to craft powerhouse copy and post it, you need to know how to track responses. Facebook, for instance, has an "Insights" tool that shows how far your words and images are reaching. Tools such as Hootsuite and Buffer track how well

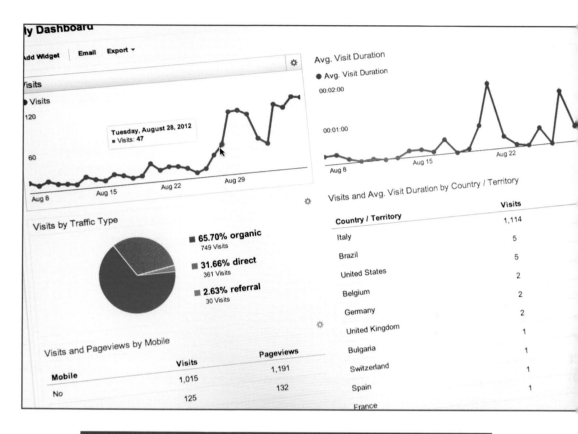

How can you determine the effectiveness of a social media campaign? Many platforms have tools that measure audience reach and response.

tweets are performing (as far as how often they are being shared or retweeted).

Social media tools can also tell how audiences are engaging with your content—did they like it, comment on it, share it, click on it, or did they just look at it? Analytics may tell you the average age range that responded best to a post, if more women responded than men, and possibly how much money the average responder earns. A very successful social media campaign may go "viral." This means that content spreads rapidly on social media through many, many shares.

WEARING MANY HATS

Sometimes, a manager will have to moderate or attend a social media "chat." A Twitter chat, for example, is an event that brings together a group of online participants who have a conversation about a topic during a set time. In some cases, it may be a chance for users to ask questions of one particular expert or celebrity. The moderator helps control the flow of the conversation and helps engage people. The more who participate, the better.

A social media pro may also have to be a blogger, producing content regularly, often like an online diary. (People blog on all sorts of topics, including fashion, fitness, food, and travel.) In addition to writing your own blog, you may devote time to responding to blogs that have something to do with your business or writing content for your company's blog. Any time users are posting, someone usually has to monitor the activity for anything offensive or inappropriate. Also, you typically have to respond to many of the reactions posted online.

Many major companies maintain popular blogs. Coca-Cola has a corporate blog that emphasizes people and emotions. Walmart has a blog featuring products, shopping tips, company history, seasonal features, and news.

Since visuals can be important for catching consumer attention, a social media job may require taking photographs, recording your own video content, or reviewing this type of content from users.

SERVING AS A SALESPERSON

Social media managers today are often acting in a similar role to salespeople or advertising experts. If Don Draper, the 1960s advertising executive from the television show *Mad Men*, were working today, he'd probably have to master social media. James Keenan, a social sales specialist, conducted a study finding that about eight out of ten salespeople using social media to sell in 2012 outperformed their peers who weren't using social media.

Learning more about sales can really help someone interested in social media, and vice versa. To one degree or another, everyone is involved with sales. If you're looking for a job, you have to sell yourself, for example. So learning effective sales techniques can help just about anyone.

Social media managers are often compelling salespeople. They typically have strong social skills and know how to engage effectively with other people.

There are many online sources that tell how to boost your sales abilities. However, the basics will always be strong communication skills, conveying passion, and winning the confidence of others.

Advertising is similar to sales because increasing sales is the ultimate goal of advertising. Those who are involved with social media may work closely with a company's advertising team on a campaign. Twitter, Facebook, LinkedIn, and other social media platforms all offer ways to advertise to a focused group of customers. As someone who works in social media, you can benefit from learning more about advertising because social media and advertising are closely related.

Customer service skills can also aid the social media moderator. When you post something in social media, you can expect a lot of responses and questions. You have to learn how to be polite, show empathy, and resolve problems.

GET SMART ON THE TECHNICAL SIDE

Most social media managers do not need in-depth technical knowledge, but some basic coding skills can make a job candidate more hirable. Coding is the set of instructions that tells computers what to do. Computer software, apps, and websites are all created with code. Code powers every social media platform. Apple cofounder Steve Jobs once said, "I think everybody in this country should learn how to program a computer because it teaches you how to think."

Not only can coding help with problem-solving skills, but it can also give a social media person a better understanding of the technology that he or she is actually using. This is a world of websites and apps, and coding makes this world tick. Effective social media depends on good design and data collection. Coding is behind both.

Coding knowledge can help if you need to work with company programmers. The website Udemy offers an entire course that teaches how to build a social networking website. People code

Learning Coding for Free

Getting a little experience in coding is incredibly valuable for anyone going into social media. There are many websites that offer free coding courses, including Codecademy. One Codecademy user went from knowing nothing about code to building one of *Time* magazine's "50 Best Websites." Codecademy teaches JavaScript, CSS, HTML, and many other languages. MIT also offers free open courseware, including "Introduction to Programming in Java" and "Introduction to Computer Science and Programming."

Another online education site, Khan Academy, provides step-by-step video tutorials. Google's University Consortium offers free courses on programming languages, as well as Android software development and web development.

Explore online to find more free instructional material or programs that may cost a small fee but give high-quality training.

using different coding languages. This course starts with the basics of coding for the web, so it covers HTML, CSS, and JavaScript languages and then goes on to other popular coding languages.

SOME COMPUTER LINGO BASICS

In 1990, computer scientist Tim Berners-Lee came up with the fundamental technologies that would form the foundation of today's internet. One of these was HTML, or hypertext markup language. This is the computer language for formatting content seen on the internet. It is called a markup language and commonly used for web design.

HTML

HTML still forms the building blocks of all websites. HTML allows a person to design a web page so it can present text, images, links, videos, interactive forms, and more. Today, XHTML is one of the newest ways for "expressing" web pages, and it is used to extend HTML. (It stands for extensible hypertext markup language.)

CSS

CSS is another essential computer language and is used hand-in-hand with HTML. CSS stands for cascading style sheets. These are instructions that "style" web pages and define how they should look in terms of fonts and colors. These sheets tell the computer or mobile browser how content should appear to the user. CSS defines layout, position, alignment, height, width, typefaces, borders, and more.

JAVASCRIPT AND OTHERS

JavaScript (or JS for short) is the computer language that adds interactivity and responsiveness to a website. It is the most popular programming language in the world. It is used together with HTML and CSS to really make things happen on screen. Animations, search boxes, payment tools, quizzes, and chat systems can all be made with JavaScript.

Some of the other top computer languages that can come into play in the social media world are C, C++, C#, Objective C, PHP, SQL, Python, and Ruby.

Without computer programming, there would be no social media. A background in coding and computer languages can be helpful.

The bottom line is that if you learn some coding, you might get ideas on how to improve functions with social media or you might even be able to one day build your own social media tool. In any case, a basic understanding of coding can help you with your job.

LEARN SEARCH ENGINE OPTIMIZATION

When you are working at a company or organization on their social media, you are trying to expand their presence on the internet and get more attention. One way to get more visitors to a website is through search engine optimization (SEO).

SEO is a process that will make a site appear high on a list of results returned by a search engine such as Google or Bing. The search engines show the viewer what is considered most important according to what the viewer is searching for. There are many techniques to improving SEO for a company or product. A few ways to improve SEO is to publish compelling content, update content regularly, and have relevant links. Using the right "keywords" can also help drive traffic to a website. As a site becomes more popular, its SEO improves, and that makes the site even more popular. So the process, in a way, feeds on itself.

Say you're the social media manager for a fashion company selling a new style of jeans. You put out announcements on Facebook, Instagram, and Twitter that generate interest in these new jeans. You post on fashion and culture blogs about your hot new product. People start sharing your posts and tweets. Bloggers hear about the new jeans and write about them. It's important that people post the link to your company website, too, because that will create more online traffic.

Suddenly, these new jeans are generating real buzz on the internet and they seem to be the hottest thing going. When someone goes to Google and types "jeans" in the search engine, guess what comes up in the first page of results? The jeans you are promoting, because you've spread the presence of these jeans on the internet and used all the right tools that increase SEO. Now more buyers are heading to the fashion company site to buy the jeans because your social media campaign led to more hits on search engines.

Chapter FOUR

Going to Work

One of the great parts of becoming a social media expert is that you can work in a field that you're really passionate about. All sorts of business are looking for professionals to handle their social media. If you're someone who loves movies, you may be the exact person to work for a film company and help them advertise their new films via social media. Or if you're someone who loves music, you might start your own business promoting bands and their upcoming shows. With the right tweets, Instagram posts, and Facebook messages, you can help musical acts build a huge following. For whatever subject interests you, there is probably a social media job out there in that field.

Business, engineering, government, fashion, high tech, and science are just a few possibilities. One example of a person finding a job that matches his interests is John Yembrick at NASA. He has been fascinated with outer space since he was a child, and he found a job that matched this passion by becoming the social media manager at NASA.

Even if you're not quite in the job market yet, you can search online and see what companies are doing for their social media. Hasbro, one of the major toy companies, features all sorts of

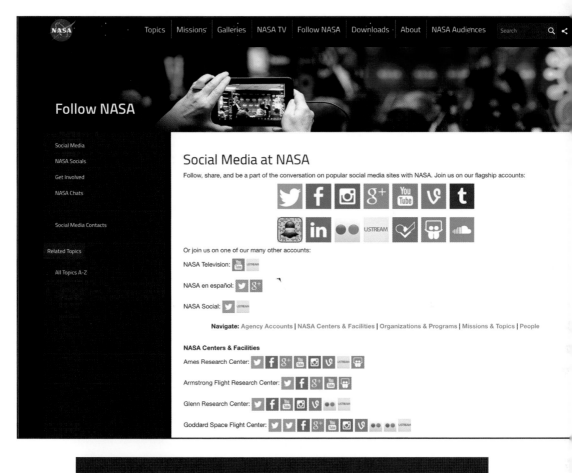

Many businesses and organizations (from the music industry to NASA to charities) depend on social media professionals.

interesting content on its Facebook page—photos of puppies with Scrabble boards, funny videos of families playing monopoly, and quiz questions. Pizza Hut's Twitter feed features deals, photos of customers, and short videos.

Think of the products you like and see how those companies are handling their social media. The energy drink Red Bull takes full advantage of the video capabilities of YouTube. In order to promote how Red Bull can get a person moving and active, the company has a YouTube channel full of athletes and daredevils doing amazing feats while skateboarding, skiing, mountain climbing, surfing, cliff diving, skydiving, and more.

HOW TO FIND YOUR DREAM JOB

After getting equipped with all the right skills, the next step is finding work. Many job websites list open positions and allow job hunters to post their résumés to make the world aware that they are searching for employment.

A few sites are dedicated to careers in technology. Dice.com specifically focuses on tech opportunities and has listed employment ads for social media specialists, social media customer service representatives, and social media gurus.

Other sites that specialize in staffing IT (information technology) professionals include Robert Half Technology, TheLadders, and Harvey Nash. The job site JobsinSocialMedia .com is strictly dedicated to opportunities in social media.

There are a number of job search engines that cover a wide range of employment possibilities and are not limited to only tech jobs. A few of the major job search tools worth checking out are Indeed.com, Simply Hired, Monster.com, CareerBuilder, and US.jobs.

Although some sites are not strictly limited to job hunting, they have sections that present job listings. Perhaps the biggest in this category is Craigslist. This is a gigantic, mostly free, classified ad site organized by locations. While employers of all sizes are using it, the ability to post ads for free easily attracts many scammers, so use it with care. Make sure any ad you respond to is legitimate. The website Mashable, which is a source for tech, digital culture, and entertainment content, also features a job board dedicated to digital and tech jobs.

BRIAN WALKER

WEB DEVELOPER

CONTACT

123-456-7890
012-345-6789

1490 General Woods,
Colorado Springs

brianwalker.co
mail@brianwalker.com

SOCIAL

---

brianwalker

brianwalker

brianwalker

Application,
Back End Developer
Datalist Co.
North Street 197,
Michigan

June 1st 2015

Dear Jonathan Westdock,

Lorem ipsum dolor sit amet, consectetur adipiscing elit. Nulla iaculis est sed erat condimentum condimentum. Ut sit amet eleifend metus. Vivamus vitae bibendum ligula, vitae auctor mauris.

Nunc eget nibh ullamcorper, maximus urna quis, sodales metus. Vivamus porttitor magna est, nec varius nisi tempus at. Nullam ipsum mauris, tempor sed ex eu, lacinia tincidunt eros. Proin fringilla nisl quis magna tempor congue.

Nulla gravida tortor eget urna volutpat, luctus placerat augue tempor. Praesent viverra nisi eget velit auctor commodo. Curabitur quis ligula ante.

Nullam scelerisque arcu non leo volutpat, a porttitor purus gravida. Duis eleifend posuere nisi, sed consectetur ante molestie viverra. Pellentesque fermentum eros ipsum.

Gravida porttitor orci pulvinar eu. Ut iaculis nibh eget nunc cursus convallis. In sit amet bibendum risus, nec hendrerit urna. Nam sit amet feugiat magna, non vulputate turpis.

Nulla gravida tortor eget urna volutpat, luctus placerat augue tempor. Praesent viverra nisi eget velit auctor commodo. Curabitur quis ligula ante.

Sincerely,

Brian Walker

Brian Walker,
Web Developer

Landing any position requires the right tools. All job hunters need a great résumé, a persuasive cover letter, like the template pictured here, and employment references.

Another great place to find social media opportunities is through social media itself. LinkedIn is specifically designed for job seekers. Profiles posted on the site are all about a person's

professional background and qualifications. The site not only helps people network with professionals who may know of opportunities, but it also features job postings. Other social media sites, such as Facebook and Twitter, can help broadcast to all your connections that you're on the hunt for work. Spreading the word is often the answer to making solid employment connections.

Many employers now search Facebook for their recruiting. Many also check social media accounts as a type of background check. An article on Job-Hunt.org says that more than 90 percent of employers and recruiters conduct a quick "background check" of job applicants using search engines. Over 70 percent of them have rejected job seekers based on inappropriate photos, comments, and content shared on Facebook. The message is: be careful what you post.

The personal interview can be key to clinching a job. Employers want to see what you are like face-to-face. Come prepared, be poised, and dress for success.

When you're seriously looking for a job, you may consider using a recruiting agency to help you as well. These are firms that help employers find the right people for the positions they are trying to fill. Check out SocialMediaHeadhunter.com, KAS Placement, and LucasGroup.com.

Apple   Yahoo!   Google Maps   YouTube   Wikipedia

http://www.linkedin.com/nhome/   LinkedIn – World's Largest Profe

Linked in ®

Home   What is LinkedIn?   Join Today   Sign In

Over 100 million professionals exchange information, ideas and

Stay informed about your contacts and i

Find the people &

One of the most popular ways today to make professional connections is through LinkedIn (www.linkedin.com), a networking website for job candidates and employers.

Also, when conducting a job hunt, keep an eye out for job fairs and conferences. These events bring together large numbers of employers and can be an ideal way to find out more about opportunities and make yourself known as well.

Big cities are the most likely places to find opportunities in social media, according to data from LinkedIn. The top cities with social media jobs are New York City, Los Angeles, San Francisco, Chicago, and London.

In this modern world where nearly everyone is online, many social media positions do not require a person to be in a particular location. Telecommuting jobs allow professionals to work from home, a café, or other locations outside of an office.

When you apply for a job, be sure you familiarize yourself with the industry and the company to which you are applying.

Tools to Land the Job

Here are the basic tools you will need to get a great job in social media. Many online sources give detailed information on how to put together each of these:

Résumé. A résumé is a summary of your skills, abilities, and accomplishments, including educational background. This is your main tool to secure a job, so it has to be error-free and well written.

(continued on the next page)

(continued from the previous page)

Cover letter. This is the letter you send to an employer along with your résumé that helps explain why you are applying for the job and why you are an ideal candidate. It's a quick sales pitch for yourself.

Recommendations and references. When employers are impressed by a candidate's résumé and cover letter, they often take the next step and call previous employers who can discuss your work history, strengths, and weaknesses. Some check them before a personal interview, and some check them after.

Interviewing skills. When an employer calls you in for an interview, you know you are a contender. Making a good impression in person is crucial. Be prepared, be on time, and always follow up with a thank-you letter or email.

The right clothes. When you do meet with human resources and other staff members of a potential employer, make sure you are dressed for success. It's often worth the investment to look sharp and dress in such a way that matches the work environment.

TYPES OF JOBS

Some of the job titles that fall under the social media heading are manager, marketer, coordinator, specialist, strategist, content editor, and consultant. No matter what the position, you're typically part of a team. Sometimes, a person in charge of social media will be called a "community manager."

The website Sprout Social says that a community manager will typically push a product, service, or brand to those who haven't heard of the business. This is called "community building." On the other hand, a social media manager may deal with people who already have a relationship with a product, service, or brand.

No matter the exact job title, professionals in this field may spend part of their day doing any of the following: responding to and helping customers, writing content, researching, strategizing,

Winning social media campaigns usually require a team effort that may bring together salespeople, designers, writers, marketers, project managers, and company leaders.

planning, evaluating performance, analyzing results, and collaborating with other company staff members. These jobs often involve a lot of monitoring, both to measure how much response is coming in and to moderate any conversations.

Social media pros may collaborate with executives, sales staff, advertising representatives, digital designers, and marketers. They work with others to strategize how to use social media to achieve set goals. The goals may be to promote a product, set up a social media advertising campaign, get customer feedback, or hold a contest.

Chapter FIVE
A Booming Field

Today, the social media universe is bigger than ever. A report by LinkedIn found that job postings for social media positions on its site grew by 1,300 percent in recent years.

The world of social media is swiftly expanding and always changing, as new online tools continue to be developed. Those who succeed have to keep up with the latest advances.

The social media landscape is constantly changing. New tools are always evolving and being introduced. In 2006, MySpace was the most popular site in the United States, but Facebook surpassed MySpace in 2009, and MySpace soon fell far behind.

Today there are more than a billion and a half users on Facebook. As users have multiplied at an astronomical rate, businesses realized the potential of connecting with customers through social media. An article in *Adweek* stated that 93 percent of marketers use social media for business, 70 percent of marketers have used Facebook successfully to gain new customers, and 34 percent have used Twitter to generate leads. The same article said that almost half of all Americans say that Facebook is their number-one influencer when it comes to making purchases. An influencer is a media source that affects people's purchasing decisions. So many people use Facebook today that it makes sense that selling products on this site has such a big impact. The power of social media is strong.

The need for social media experts expands beyond the realm of business. Schools, universities, hospitals, government agencies, nonprofits, social awareness groups, charities, and political campaigns have all recognized the power of social media. So if you're deep into using Facebook, Snapchat, YouTube, Twitter, or any of these types of platforms, your interest and skills may translate into a rewarding job path.

One of the keys to succeeding as a social media manager is being able to adapt. Today's professionals are often transforming as the world changes. They must keep up with all the latest tools. In this field, you have to be able to reinvent yourself.

To become a strong job candidate, you have to always acquire new skills and continually hone and refine your writing. Diversified skills provide a backup if trends change. Some predict that there may one day be a social media backlash—people may get tired

Standing Out in a Crowded Field

The number of people trying to gain attention on social media seems infinite. It's hard to stand out from the ever-expanding pack. You have to keep thinking more and more creatively. Here are a few quick examples of people who found ways to grab attention on social media.

From homeless to Vine sensation. Jérôme Jarre, age twenty-four, was homeless in New York City. He secretly slept on an office floor and showered in a nearby gym. Then he found the power of the six-second video format on Vine, the social media site that features extremely short videos. He made videos (or "Vines") of himself hugging people in the street, hanging out with a squirrel, and more. In a short time, he had eight million followers.

Crazy socks catch fire. Social media strategist Ted Rubin had always loved to wear wild socks. One day a friend asked if she could take a photo of his socks and post it to Twitter. People were curious about his socks and wondered what he wears each day. So Rubin started posting sock pictures on a regular basis. He became known on Twitter as the crazy sock guy. The gimmick helped him to build a brand, and he gained tons of followers.

(continued from the previous page)

The ALS ice bucket challenge. To raise money and awareness about ALS (amyotrophic lateral sclerosis) or Lou Gehrig's disease, Pete Frates, a twenty-nine-year-old Boston College baseball star with ALS, came up with the idea of dumping ice water over a person's head as way to get attention. His large network of friends and family filmed themselves dousing themselves in ice water and posted the videos to Facebook. Participants soared, social media postings went viral, and donations to the ALS Association skyrocketed.

Never underestimate the power of pets. When Virgin America Airlines learned that a very cute Pomeranian dog named Boo had close to five million followers, it saw a way to get publicity. Virgin prides itself on being pet friendly, so it enlisted Boo to be its official pet liaison. Today, Boo has more than seventeen million fans and Virgin has won the hearts— and business— of dog-loving travelers.

of having their faces buried in devices and crave old-fashioned human interaction. The message is: be prepared for change. No matter what trends come, writing will always be a valuable skill to have. Always aim to build a track record of success because that usually leads to more success.

NEW TECHNOLOGIES AND USES

The tech world recently saw the launch of a number of live video-streaming platforms, including Periscope, Meerkat, Blab, Google Hangouts, and Facebook Mentions. With Facebook Mentions,

The live video streaming platform Periscope allows users to video-record and broadcast anywhere in the world. It's one example of how social media tools are evolving.

you can tell your story as it happens with live video. While the technology is relatively new, businesses can use the tool to conduct a real-time Q&A, presentation, or tour. YouNow is an expanding live-stream broadcast site that is very popular with young people.

Social media as a tool among coworkers is still a relatively new idea. Recently, Facebook launched Facebook at Work. The program is dedicated to allowing coworkers to better communicate with one another in the workplace. It separates a

person's online work life from his or her personal life.

Slack is a related software. This instant messaging and collaboration system started just a few years ago. Teams of coworkers can communicate, work on projects together, and share links, photos, and more in real time. If you think you might pursue a social media career, be sure to look into these new tools.

Right now social media thrives on sharing personal experiences. Some people envision a future where users will share physical senses. Far in the future, devices that connect us to the internet may be implanted in our bodies. In an interview in *Vanity Fair* magazine, Facebook

People today spend long stretches of time staring at screens, and that time is only expected to grow as social media tools spread to the workplace and offer more functions.

cofounder Mark Zuckerberg said, "Eventually I think we're going to have technology where we can communicate our full sensory experience and emotions to someone through thought."

Data collection is one of the major services offered by social media sites, and it's expected to grow even bigger. Social media sites are able to collect data on users—what their likes and dislikes are, how much they earn, where they live, etc. Companies are able to gather more and more knowledge of customers and their interests. That way they can target their social media campaigns to very specific people. In the near future, there might even be geographic tracking of customers, so if you're walking past a Starbucks, for instance, you might suddenly get a tweet for a deal on a cup of coffee. Starbucks might use geographic location technology to know exactly where their customers are and offer them deals on the spot.

STEPPING INTO THE VIRTUAL WORLD

Recently, tech companies have been developing and refining virtual reality (VR) technology. By wearing special headsets and sometimes gloves with built-in sensors, a person can totally immerse themselves in a 3D, computer-generated world.

As a young teen, Palmer Luckey became obsessed with developing an ideal VR system. He developed a state-of-the-art virtual reality system called Oculus Rift. He sold his company to Facebook for $2 billion.

When Facebook bought Oculus Rift, people speculated how social media and virtual reality might be combined. Soon after, Facebook introduced an app called Oculus Social Alpha. Through the app, users can join others in a virtual movie theater to watch a film. Those who enter the theater are represented by an avatar,

Recent innovations in virtual reality technology are allowing people to interact with each other in 3D virtual worlds, taking social media to a whole new dimension.

a graphical representation of a user. The technology shows the potential for how people can interact in a virtual universe.

Some experts envision a world where VR users can choose a virtual persona and then jump from virtual space to virtual space and interact socially with other people. In the future, you may be stepping into a social media world where you feel like you're having a conversation with another person and even making eye contact, but in reality you're sitting home alone wearing a VR headset.

Google is selling low-cost VR goggles for under $15. People are intrigued by this new VR technology and spend a lot of time with it. Businesses have their eye on developing VR content because it has the potential to attract attention and build interest.

New developments such as VR will always be a part of the technology world, and social media is continually looking for ways to combine forces with the latest technological advances. To be successful in this field, you have to stay informed and keep learning. The fact that technology is always changing is what makes it exciting.

Today, social media is essential, fast-paced, and fun. Social media experts bring people together and build communities. The technology is also giving a voice to more and more people across the globe. Amy Jo Martin, author, speaker, entrepreneur, and founder and CEO of Digital Royalty, said, "Social media is the ultimate equalizer. It gives a voice and a platform to anyone willing to engage."

Glossary

analytics The systematic study of data or statistics.

Android An operating system for smartphones and other devices, developed by Android, Inc., and later bought by Google.

app Short for application, especially one that can be downloaded to a mobile device.

blogging A web log or a chronological log of text or other media presented on a web page.

bookmarking Saving addresses of internet pages so you can find them again and sometimes share them.

browser A computer program that lets internet users see, access, and navigate the web. Common browsers are Internet Explorer, Google Chrome, Mozilla Firefox, and Apple Safari.

chat Any kind of communication over the internet that offers real-time sending and receiving of text messages.

crowdsourcing The process of getting needed services, ideas, content, or money by reaching out to a large group online.

hashtag The # symbol, called a hashtag, is used to mark keywords or topics in a tweet.

interactive Providing a two-way flow of information between a computer and computer user.

marketing The activities of promoting and selling services and products. Marketing is everything done to reach and persuade potential customers, as opposed to sales, which is everything done to make the actual sale.

search engine A website, such as Google or Bing, that searches the internet for content.

search engine optimization (SEO) The process of maximizing the number of visitors to a website by taking actions that will make the site appear high on the list of results given by a search engine.

social media platform A web-based operating system that allows the use, management, and development of social media.

soft skills General work and people skills that apply to all jobs, such as the ability to collaborate, accept feedback, and manage time.

stats Short for statistics, or a large amount of numerical data collected to be analyzed and interpreted.

tweet To post information on the social media site Twitter.

video-streaming Sending video content over the internet to be viewed in real time, meaning not downloaded to be viewed later.

wiki A website that allows collaborative editing.

For More Information

American Marketing Association (AMA)
130 E. Randolph Street, 22nd Floor
Chicago, IL 60601
(800) AMA-1150
Website: https://www.ama.org

The AMA covers all aspects of marketing, including social
    media. The association has provided seminars such as
    "Essentials of Social Marketing" and "Advanced Social
    Media."

Canada Business Network
6081 Number 3 Road, #610
Richmond, BC V6Y 2B2
Canada
(604) 713-8383
Website: http://www.canadabusiness.ca

This organization provides Canadian businesses with resources
    they need to grow and prosper, including articles such as
    "The Pros and Cons of Social Media" and "How to Use
    Social Media to Reach Your Customers."

Canadian Internet Marketing Association
2 St. Clair Avenue, W, #602
Toronto, ON M4V 1L5
Canada
(416) 598-3400
Website: http://www.internetmarketingassociation.ca

This professional group for internet marketers in Canada offers
    material concerning social media issues.

Common Sense Media
650 Townsend, Suite 435
San Francisco, CA 94103
(415) 863-0600
Website: https://www.commonsensemedia.org

This site rates, educates, and advocates for kids, families, and
schools. It also features content related to social media,
such as "16 Apps and Websites Kids Are Heading to After
Facebook."

International Social Marketing Association
6414 Hollins Drive
Bethesda, MD 20817
(301) 581-2422
Website: http://www.i-socialmarketing.org

This professional group offers blogs, webinars, events, and
other tools to help those in the field of social marketing.

Social Media Club
Global Headquarters
PO Box 14881
San Francisco, CA, 94114-0881
Website: http://socialmediaclub.org

Social Media Club's mission is to promote media literacy,
promote standard technologies, encourage ethical behavior,
and share best practices. Members share their knowledge
of social media.

WEBSITES

Because of the changing nature of internet links, Rosen Publishing has developed an online list of websites related to the subject of this book. This site is updated regularly. Please use this link to access the list:

http://www.rosenlinks.com/TTHIC/media

For Further Reading

Abram, Carolyn. *Facebook for Dummies.* Hoboken, NJ: Wiley, 2013.

Baer, Jay. *Youtility: Why Smart Marketing Is About Help Not Hype.* New York, NY: Penguin, 2014.

Boyd, Danah. *It's Complicated: The Social Lives of Networked Teens.* New Haven, CT: Yale University Press, 2015.

Coine, Ted. *A World Gone Social.* New York, NY: AMACOM, 2014.

Elad, Joel. *LinkedIn for Dummies*. Hoboken, NJ: Wiley, 2014.

Fitton, Laura. *Twitter for Dummies.* Hoboken, NJ: Wiley, 2014.

Handley, Ann. *Everybody Writes: Your Go-To Guide to Creating Ridiculously Good Content.* Hoboken, NJ: Wiley, 2014.

Holiday, Ryan. *Growth Hacker Marketing: A Primer on the Future of PR, Marketing, and Advertising.* New York, NY: Penguin, 2014.

Hyatt, Michael. *Platform: Get Noticed in a Noisy World.* Nashville, TN: Thomas Nelson, 2012.

Kawaski, Guy. *The Art of Social Media: Power Tips for Power Users.* New York, NY: Penguin, 2014.

Mansfield, Heather. *Social Media for Social Good: A How-To Guide for Nonprofits*. New York, NY: McGraw-Hill, 2011.

Rowell, Rebecca. *Social Media: Like It or Leave It.* North Mankato, MN: Compass Point Books, 2015.

Schaefer, Mark. *Born to Blog: Building Your Blog for Personal and Business Success One Post at a Time.* New York, NY: McGraw-Hill, 2013.

Standage, Tom. *Writing on the Wall: Social Media—The First 2,000 Years.* New York, NY: Bloomsbury USA, 2014.

Vaynerchuk, Gary. *Jab, Jab, Jab, Right Hook: How to Tell Your Story in a Noisy Social World.* New York, NY: HarperBusiness, 2013.

Waldman, Joshua. *Job Searching with Social Media for Dummies*. Hoboken, NJ: Wiley, 2013.

Bibliography

Abernathy, Jennifer. *The Complete Idiot's Guide to Social Marketing*. New York, NY: Penguin, 2012.

Ayres, Scott. "How to Become a Social Media Manager in Six Easy Steps." PostPlanner. Retrieved April 24, 2016. https://www.postplanner.com/how-to-become-a-social-media-manager-in-6-steps/.

Davis, Kathleen. "The Rise of Social Media as a Career." Entrepreneur, October 1, 2013. https://www.entrepreneur.com/article/228651.

DeMyers, Jason. "7 Social Media Platforms That Could Explode Before 2016." *Forbes*, August 13, 2015. http://www.forbes.com.

Dugan, Lauren. "Twitter Basics: Why 140-Characters, and How to Write More." *Adweek*, November 11, 2011. http://www.adweek.com.

"History of the Web." World Wide Web Foundation. Retrieved April 24, 2016. http://webfoundation.org/about/vision/history-of-the-web/.

Holiday, Ryan. "How to Host a Successful Reddit AMA." Mashable, March 25, 2013. http://www.mashable.com.

Jones, Alex. "Study: 78% of Salespeople Using Social Media Outsell Their Peers." Social Horsepower, April 5, 2015. https://www.socialhp.com/blog/study-78-of-salespeople-using-social-media-outsell-their-peers/.

Joyce, Susan. "A Guide to Facebook for Job Search." Job-Hunt. Retrieved April 24, 2016. http://www.job-hunt.org/social-networking/facebook-job-search/facebook-job-search.shtml.

Kaban, Shama. *The Zen of Social Marketing: An Easier Way to Build Credibility, Generate Buzz, and Increase Revenue*. Dallas, TX: BenBella Books, 2013.

Lenhart, Amanda. "Teens, Social Media & Technology Overview." The Pew Center, April 9, 2015. http://www .pewinternet.org/2015/04/09/teens-social-media-technology -2015/.

Lynley, Matthew. "With 100 People Watching Vine Videos Every Month, Jason Mante Says Monetization Still Isn't the Focus." TechCrunch, May 5, 2015. http://techcrunch.com.

"The Online High School Program to Master the Language of Today: Social Media." Virtual Learning Academy. Retrieved April 24, 2016. http://vlacs.org/online-high-school-program -social-media/.

Patterson, Michael. "Social Media Manager Vs. Community Manager: What's the Difference?" Sprout Social, October 30, 2014. http://sproutsocial.com/insights/social-media -vs-community-manager/.

"Reach of Leading Social Media and Networking Sites Used by Teenagers and Young People in the United States as of February 2016." Statista: The Statistics Portal. Retrieved April 24, 2016. http://www.statista.com.

Safko, Lon, and David Brake. *The Social Media Bible: Tactics, Tools, & Strategies for Business Success*. Hoboken, NJ: Wiley, 2009.

"Social Media, Social Life: How Teens View Their Digital Lives." A Common Sense Research Study, June 26, 2012. https:// www.commonsensemedia.org.

Vaynerchuk, Gary. "The Snapchat Generation: A Guide to Snapchat's History." Retrieved April 24, 2016. http://www. garyvaynerchuk.com/the-snap-generation-a-guide-to -snapchats-history/.

Wellons, Mary Catherine. "11 Predictions on the Future of Social Media." CNBC. Retrieved April 24, 2016. http://www. cnbc.com/2014/10/02/11-predictions-on-the-future-of- social-media.html.

Yembrick, John. Interview with the author, April 20, 2016.

Index

A

B

C

D

E

F

G

W

Y

Z

ABOUT THE AUTHOR

Don Rauf is the author of several technology books for young people, including *Kickstarter*, *Killer Lipstick and Other Spy Gadgets*, *Virtual Reality*, *Getting the Most Out of Makerspaces to Explore Arduino & Electronics*, *Getting the Most Out of Makerspaces to Build Unmanned Aerial Vehicles*, and *Powering Up a Career in Internet Security*.

PHOTO CREDITS